SERMON OUTLINES ON MEN OF THE BIBLE

Charles R. Wood

KREGEL PUBLICATIONS
Grand Rapids, Michigan 49501

Sermon Outlines on Men of the Bible, by Charles R. Wood. © 1990 by Kregel Publications, a division of Kregel, Inc., P. O. Box 2607, Grand Rapids, MI 49501. All rights reserved.

Cover: Don Ellens

Library of Congress Cataloging-in-Publication Data

Wood, Charles R. (Charles Robert), 1933–
Sermon outlines on men of the Bible / Charles R. Wood.
    p.   cm.—(Easy-to-use sermon outline series)

1. Bible—Biography—Sermons—Outlines, syllabi, etc. I. Title. II. Series: Wood, Charles R. (Charles Robert), 1933-   Easy-to-use sermon outline series.

BS571.2.W66   1990   251'.02—dc20   90-38573
                                                                   CIP
ISBN 0-8254-3988-4 (pbk.)

1 2 3 4 5 Printing/Year 94 93 92 91 90

Printed in the United States of America

Contents

Introduction 5
Abraham: When Faith Falters— *Genesis 12:10-20* 7
Lot and His Losses— *Genesis 13:5-13* 9
Esau: A Careless Man's Foolish Bargain— *Genesis 25:27-34* 10
Abraham's Servant: In the Way— *Genesis 24* 11
Balaam: What Was, Still Is— *Numbers 22:2-41* 13
Joshua: The Man Who Walked by Faith— *Joshua 1:8* 15
Samuel: The Making of a Man— *1 Samuel 2, 3* 17
What Happened to Saul?— *1 Samuel* 19
Samuel's Swan Song— *1 Samuel 12:1-25* 21
Jonathan: The Man Who Defines Character— *1 Samuel 18, 19, 20* .23
David's Great Sin— *2 Samuel 11:1-5* 25
Adonijah: Going My Way— *1 Kings 1:5-9* 27
Solomon: Not Fully After the Lord— *1 Kings 3:11-14; 4:29-34; 11:1-8* 29
Jeroboam the Determined— *1 Kings 11:26—14:20* 31
Elijah and God's Tender, Loving Care— *1 Kings 19:4-8* 33
Elisha: Let Thy Mantle Fall on Me— *1 Kings 19:19-21* 35
Ahab the Average— *1 Kings 20, 21* 37
Jabez: A Man More Honorable— *1 Chronicles 4:9, 10* 39
John the Baptist: Man, Ministry, Message— *Mark 1:1-15* 40
Good King Hezekiah— *2 Chronicles 31:20, 21* 41
Josiah the Tenderhearted— *2 Chronicles 34, 35* 43
Ezra: The Man With the Right Heart— *Ezra 7:1-28* 45
The Rich Young Ruler— *Mark 10:17-22; 1 Timothy 6:6-10, 17-19* ..47
Simeon's Spiritual Secrets— *Luke 2:21-38* 49
The Prodigal Son— *Luke 15* 51
That Older Brother— *Luke 15:24-32* 53
John the Apostle: Old Man of the Faith— *John 1:1-14* 55
In the Trail of Thomas— *John 20:24-29* 56

The Man Born Blind: Now I Can See— *John 9:25* 57
Judas: The Man Who Gave Traitors a Bad Name— *John 13:21-30* .59
Cornelius: The Missing Ingredient— *Acts 10* 61
Timothy: The Really Important Things— *1 Timothy 4:12* 63

Textual Index

Genesis 12:10-20 7	1 Kings 20, 21 37
Genesis 13:5-13 9	1 Chronicles 4:9, 10 39
Genesis 24 11	2 Chronicles 31:20, 21 41
Genesis 25:27-34 10	2 Chronicles 34, 35 43
Numbers 22:2-41 13	Ezra 7:1-28 45
Joshua 1:8 15	Mark 1:1-15 40
1 Samuel 19	Mark 10:17-22 47
1 Samuel 2, 3 17	Luke 2:21-38 49
1 Samuel 12:1-25 21	Luke 15 51
1 Samuel 18, 19, 20 23	Luke 15:24-32 53
2 Samuel 11:1-5 21	John 1:1-14 55
1 Kings 1:5-9 27	John 9:25 57
1 Kings 3:11-14 29	John 13:21-30 59
1 Kings 4:29-34 29	Acts 10 61
1 Kings 11:1-8 29	John 20:24-29 56
1 Kings 11:26—14:20 31	1 Timothy 4:12 63
1 Kings 19:4-8 33	1 Timothy 6:6-10, 17-19 47
1 Kings 19:19-21 35	

Introduction

The pages of Scripture abound with the fascinating stories of real people. As much flesh and blood as you and I, their stories reveal the same foibles and failures as well as strengths and successes that mark our contemporary lives. As we explore their lives in depth, we discover that ancient times were marked by conditions and circumstances not all that unlike modern days.

Careful investigation of the biblical record reveals not only specific similarities to ourselves, but also changeless principles regarding human nature, interpersonal relationships, the ways of God in dealing with man, and the obligations of man in relationship to his God. No man who will diligently study biblical biographies need ever remain ignorant of the essential truths necessary to understand and to assist one's community of peers.

The study of biblical biography has been an enjoyable occupation of the compiler of this book during more than thirty years of pastoral ministry, and the sermons that have arisen from these studies have been enthusiastically received by four different congregations. Each of the messages in this compilation has been preached to a local church congregation, and each outline has then been carefully revised for publication.

It would be possible to preach most of these messages with little or no preparation, but their expository nature and principle basis are such that careful preparation should pay dividends out of proportion to the time invested. The Scripture portion on which the message is based should be read and reread, and the outline itself subjected to careful scrutiny.

These outlines are designed to be thought-provoking and stimulating rather than definitive and limiting. One should feel totally free to alter any message to conform to his own style of thinking, organization and presentation, and it is altogether possible that a portion of a sermon may be deemed a sufficient basis for an entire message or that one of my sermons may become several in your hands.

There is one overarching consideration that demands mention in a day of careless exposition and indifferent hermeneutics: the Bible means what it means and not what we want it to mean, wish it meant, or even need it to mean to support some personally proffered position. As has been true throughout church history, the true preacher of the Word is bound by the Word. So be it!

From the heart of a preacher with a heart for preachers comes this series of suggested and fully-formed messages. May the Lord who shaped the lives of the men about whom we preach be pleased to bless both preachers and preaching so that "the dead may live" both from the pages of Scripture and among those to whom we preach.

Abraham: When Faith Falters
Genesis 12:10-20

Introduction

Abraham has been called from Ur through Haran. He is now in Palestine, and things begin to happen.

I. **The Setting**
   A. Abraham is in the place of God's choosing.
      1. Has settled down.
      2. Famine strikes.
      3. Shows that trouble can come even when we are in God's will—not everything bad is punishment.
   B. Abraham turns to Egypt for support.
      1. Common practice.
      2. Debatable solution.
      3. Proved disastrous.

II. **The Sin**
   A. Abraham's fear.
      1. Attractiveness of Sarah (65 years old).
      2. Cultural situation in Egypt saw beauty in older woman.
   B. Abraham's solution.
      1. Encourages a lie (only half-truth).
      2. Risks the dissolution of God's promise.
      3. Puts Sarah on the line for self (would sacrifice her honor).
   C. Abraham's sin.
      1. Simply does not trust God's ability to keep.
      2. Really a failure of faith.
   D. Abraham's deliverance.
      1. God intervenes to deliver Pharoah.
      2. God intervenes to maintain His purposes.

III. **The Sequel**
   Abraham's act triggered a chain of events which would later cost him much. What did Abraham's sin do?
   A. It grieved God. Sin always grieves God (Eph. 4:30).
   B. It cost him his testimony.
      1. Pharoah reproached him.
      2. He may well have borne evil influence on Lot.
      3. Sin always costs lost testimony.
   C. It weakened his own faith.
      1. He failed God later by doing the same thing (Gen. 20).
      2. Did so a second time in spite of first experience.

    3. Once sin occurs, the second time is much simpler (sinful patterns are easy to establish).
  D. It weakened the faith of Sarah.
    1. He was head of household in God's economy.
    2. Sarah later laughed in disbelief at God's promise.
    3. Our sins often weaken the faith of others, especially our children.
  E. It caused Pharoah to be afflicted (v. 17).
    1. It is possible for the sins of Christians to hurt others.
    2. Tragic that rebuke (vv. 18, 19) came from ungodly.
  F. It resulted in contact with Hagar (16:3).
    1. Evidently added her to household.
    2. She later became mistress with tragic results.
    3. Once into sin, sins are more accessible.
  G. It provided a bad example for Isaac.
    1. Son did just what father did (Gen. 26).
    2. No doubt he had been told about act.

Conclusion

There are several important principles in this passage:
- Sin has its price.
- Sin always results in lost testimony.
- Sin always makes it easier for more sin.
- Sin always affects others (Christian and non-Christians).
- Sin always grieves God.

Lot and His Losses
Genesis 13: 5-13

Introduction

The decisions of life are of greatest importance and must be made with the utmost of care. Lot amply illustrates this truth.

I. **Lot Was a Good Man**
   A. Family background.
   B. Cast his lot with Abraham.
      1. Left Haran.
      2. Left Egypt.
   C. Capable enough to handle prosperity.

II. **Lot Made a Foolish Choice**
   A. Reason for it: burgeoning prosperity.
   B. Possibility for it: Abraham graciously yielded.
   C. Motivation for it: desire for what seemed best—latent desire for world.

III. **Lot Lost a Great Deal**
   A. Captured in raid (v. 14).
      1. Abraham delivered him.
      2. Failed to take the warning.
   B. Lost his influence.
      1. Shown in the scene with the angelic visitors (19:1-11).
      2. Shown in his inability to move his family (19:13, 14, 26).
   C. Lost all his possessions in fleeing—chose this direction for possessions sake.
   D. Lost his morality (19:30-32). What he had maintained in Sodom, he lost to his own daughter.

IV. **Lot Would Teach Us Some Lesson**
   A. The importance of decisions.
      1. Seemed insignificant.
      2. His was favor of the world over approval of God.
   B. Decisions should be faced carefully.
      1. Examine motives.
      2. Investigate God's will.

Conclusion

The decisions of life are so important. It is possible to lose much through foolish choices that look good.

Esau: A Careless Man's Foolish Bargain
Genesis 25:27-34

Introduction
One can learn so much from short passages in Scripture. The character of two men is specially revealed in this brief story.

I. **Unfortunate Impatience With God's Program**
   A. Jacob knew what God planned to do.
      1. Clearly revealed to Rebekah (25:23-26).
      2. Doubtlessly revealed to Jacob by Rebekah.
   B. Jacob chose to handle it his own way.
      1. Something mean and base about Jacob.
      2. Jacob sought a good end but used wrong means.
   C. Jacob really lost out as a result.
      1. He had to flee and couldn't enjoy gain.
      2. On return, forced to honor Esau.
      3. Had to wait for Esau's surrender of land (faith involves living without scheming).

II. **Tragic Indifference Toward Relating Values**
   Jacob looks bad, but Esau comes out worse: (v. 34, Heb. 12:6).
   A. The nature of the birthright.
      1. Succession to the earthly inheritance of Canaan.
      2. Possession of covenant blessing.
      3. Privilege of place in line of promised seed.
   B. The nature of the swap.
      1. He was hungry: "I'm dying of hunger."
      2. Birthright probably discussed before.
      3. Jacob drives a hard bargain.
      4. Esau's acquiescence interesting: I prefer present gratifications to deferred benefits.
      5. Jacob smart enough to get an oath.
   C. The flaw in Esau's evaluations.
      1. He valued the seen over the unseen.
      2. He valued the temporary more than the permanent.
      3. He valued the material ahead of the spiritual.
      4. He sacrificed the permanent on the altar of the immediate.

Conclusion
We prefer illusions to realities, we choose time rather than eternity, and we take the pleasures of sin for a season rather than enjoying the blessings of God forever. How much of the spirit of Esau is there in you?

Abraham's Servant: In the Way
Genesis 24

Introduction

We say to a child, "You're always in the way." That means underfoot, blocking progress, jamming traffic—that is bad, but it isn't always bad to be "in the way." Consider the servant of Abraham.

I. **He Had an Enormous Challenge (vv. 1-9)**
   A. Abraham had desires.
      1. Don't want Canaanite wife for Isaac.
      2. Go to my home country and get wife.
   B. Abraham gave directions.
      1. Told him where to go and what to do.
      2. Gave him release if he did what he was told without success.
   C. Abraham demanded dedication—hand under the thigh.

II. **He Had Singular Success**
   A. He devised a plan (vv. 10-14).
   B. He saw it work (vv. 15-21).
   C. He followed up on it (vv. 22-25, 28-33).
   D. He was faithful to his task (vv. 24-49, esp. 33).
   E. He completed what he set out to do (vv. 50-61).
   F. He saw complete success (vv. 62-67).

III. **He Had a Simple Secret**
   A. Throughout, he seeks God's face (vv. 12-14, 42-44).
   B. Throughout, he follows God's leading (vv. 21, 49).
   C. Throughout, he gives credit to the Lord (vv. 26, 27*a*, 48, 52, 56).
   D. But ultimate secret lies in v. 27*b*. He was doing what he was supposed to be doing, and thus God blessed him.

IV. **He Taught a Valuable Lesson**
   The blessing of the Lord is most likely to fall on those who are serving Him!
   A. Our misunderstanding.
      1. We believe God is unconditionally obligated to answer prayer.
      2. We believe obedience is totally passive.
   B. The proper approach.
      1. God's blessing rests on obedience.
      2. Amply illustrated from life.
   C. The challenge.
      1. Are you seeing the blessings you wish?

2. Are you serving as you ought?
3. Are you frustrating the grace of God?

Conclusion

God is pouring out His blessing; are you "in the way"? Is that why you have not known more blessing?

Balaam: What Was, Still Is
Numbers 22:2-41

Introduction

Balaam was bad news, but he does show us many things to avoid in our own lives. He had a character quality which is very common—that of wanting his own way no matter what. He went after his own way despite the will of God, and he thus shows the danger of self-will when it comes to spiritual things.

I. **The Decision He Faced**
   A. He was asked to perform a very specific task:
      1. To curse a nation [he reveals his knowledge of the real issues in his prayer] (vv. 9-11).
      2. He knew exactly what the issues were in his invitation to serve Balak.
   B. He also knew that what he was asked to do was wrong.
      1. He knew in his conscience, doubtlessly, before he even took the matter to God.
      2. Once he took the matter to God, he knew by direct revelation that it was wrong (v. 12).
         a. This is a key element in the story.
         b. His knowledge was such that he was condemned by his own mouth (23:19).
   C. He faced great enticements.
      1. He was lured with money, prestige, power.
      2. The person promising could produce.
   D. He is strikingly like us.
      1. He is faced with a choice between right and wrong.
      2. He clearly knows which is which.
      3. The inducements are mostly on the side of doing what is wrong.

II. **The Determination He Revealed**
   A. He was perplexed.
      1. He knew he could not successfully go against the Word of God.
      2. He very much wanted what was offered.
   B. He was persistent.
      1. He went to God and got his answer.
      2. He gave an answer to the messengers.
      3. He went back to God on an issue that was already settled for him (v. 12).
      4. He tried to move God on his return visit.
         a. He tried to make what was wrong yesterday, right today.

        b. He failed to realize that when God says no, the answer is no.
        c. This explains vv. 20 and 21.
        d. It also explains his exchange with the angel (v. 34*b*).
  C. He was permitted.
    1. God said, "Go ahead."
    2. God will sometimes allow us to go in our own way if we are determined.
  D. Again he is very much like us.
    1. He wanted what he wanted.
    2. He wanted it badly enough to try to change God's mind on it.
    3. He wanted it badly enough to go against the will of the Lord on the matter (when you want to do something badly enough, you can always find some excuse to do it).

III. The Disaster He Caused
  A. He really was not able to hurt the cause of God.
    1. God would not allow him to do so.
    2. He was forced to do the opposite of what he wanted to do.
  B. He made a mess for himself.
    1. God's purposes prevailed.
    2. He was hardened in his purposes.
    3. He suffered loss for his trouble.
  C. He ended up paying for his disobedience—dearly.
    1. He went on for a fairly long time.
    2. Ultimately, his sin came back to rest upon him in death.
  D. He teaches us a valuable lesson.
    1. You cannot successfully go against God.
    2. Ultimately there is a price for going against the Word of God.

Conclusion

We are constantly faced with right and wrong decisions, and we are always being enticed to do the wrong. We try to make the wrong right, but God does not change His mind. What you believed was wrong—if your belief was based on Scripture—is still wrong. Find the will of God in the Word of God and stick to it no matter what may happen.

Joshua: The Man Who Walked by Faith
Joshua 1:8

Introduction

Joshua fit the battle of Jericho ... And he did a lot of other things as well. In fact, he is one of the towering figures of the Old Testament.

I. **Joshua's Success**
   A. He was a success as a follower.
      1. Always somewhere around Moses.
      2. Present where Moses' own sons should have been.
   B. He was a success as a spy.
      1. Understood the commission.
      2. Gained great reward for his success.
   C. He was a success as a leader.
      1. Led nation for many years.
      2. Had less trouble doing so than Moses did.
   D. He was a success as a general.
      1. Made Israel a force to be reckoned with.
      2. Had an excellent military plan.
   E. He was a success as a household head.
      1. "As for me and my house..."
      2. Said at a time when everyone knew it was true.

II. **Joshua's Secret (1:8)**
   A. He was promised prosperity and success.
   B. He was given the ingredients for it.
      1. Don't let the Book get away from you.
      2. Meditate on it (know what it says and what it means).
      3. Observe to do all that is in it.
   C. He was cautioned about the difficulties on the pathway to success (vv. 6, 7, 9).

III. **Joshua's Slip**
   A. One recorded mistake—the Gibeonite league.
   B. The story.
      1. Gibeonites came deceitfully.
      2. Joshua bought the deceit because he failed to consult the Lord (9:14).
   C. The mistake was made because.
      1. The story appeared plausible.
      2. They looked legitimate.
      3. The situation seemed positive.
      4. There weren't any negative factors.

D. The mistake plagued him the rest of the time he led Israel.
   1. Eroded his authority.
   2. Set the pace of later actions.
   3. Kept a compromise living among them.

Conclusion

Joshua was successful in all, well, almost all he did. That success was traceable to simple obedience to the Word of God. The one exception was painful.
- It plagued him throughout life.
- It came because he acted on appearances.
- It came because he failed to go to the Book for direction.

Your ultimate success will be determined by your adherence to the Book. Have you committed to obedience? What are you doing that you have not checked with the Bible?

Samuel: The Making of a Man
1 Samuel 2, 3

Introduction

Seven verses speak of Samuel's early life (2:11, 18, 21, 26; 3:1, 7, 19). In the last three, he was doing well when there was no word from the Lord (3:1); he was doing well when he had not even heard from the Lord personally (3:7); and he was blessed at a time when everything was falling apart around him (3:19). From this, there are some lessons to be learned.

I. **Perfecting Practice Is More Important Than Professing Perfection**
   A. Eli did a terrible job with his own sons but a good job with Samuel—many possible reasons.
      1. Learned from bad experiences.
      2. Gave Samuel counsel that he should have followed himself.
   B. Eli was guilty of:
      1. Knowing more than he did.
      2. Teaching others what he could not do himself.
      3. Expecting from others what he did not expect from himself.
   C. He provides a caution.
      1. Most of us talk better than we walk.
      2. Most of us can tell others what to do better than we can do it ourselves.
      3. Most of us have a desperate need to keep our walk lined up with our talk.

II. **The Direction of the Day Doesn't Determine the Destiny of a Man**
   A. Samuel grew up in terrible days.
      1. Conditions—even in religion—were awful.
      2. Samuel was in the midst of the mess.
      3. Samuel had every excuse that any man has ever had to live badly.
   B. Samuel was a model of what a man should be.
      1. He lived straight and pure.
      2. He did what was right.
      3. He knew the special favor of the Lord.
   C. There is a special lesson for us here.
      1. We live in a very evil day in society and in Christianity.
      2. We have a tendency to be affected by it and to excuse ourselves.
      3. The direction of the day is no excuse at all.

III. **A Submissive Spirit Is the Secret of Spiritual Success (3:1-10)**
   A. Samuel was a good example.
      1. He lived by what he professed.
      2. He was able to go straight when all around were crooked.
   B. There is a secret to his success.
      1. Shown early in life—"Speak, Lord, for thy servant heareth".
      2. Throughout life Samuel showed a sensitivity to the Word of the Lord and a willingness to do it.
   C. This is a lesson to us.
      1. Sensitivity and submission to the Word will solve the preaching/practicing dilemma.
      2. Sensitivity and submission to the Word will enable living against the direction of the day.
      3. There is no spiritual success without this basic element.

Conclusion

We wouldn't have the problems we do if we would settle the issue of our relationship to the Word of the Lord as Samuel did.

What Happened to Saul?
1 Samuel

Introduction

There is no stranger, sadder story in all of Scripture than that of Saul. Few ever fell from higher to lower. Few ever wasted more potential. Few ever ended more tragically. What in the world happened to Saul?

I. **The Course of His Conduct**
    A. Good beginnings.
        1. Portrait of a very fine man (humble, brave, submissive, thoughtful, big-hearted).
        2. Unspotted by the immoralities of contemporaries.
        3. Resolved to govern in the name of Jehovah.
        4. God even gave him a "new" heart.
    B. A pattern of backsliding.
        1. The foolish steps.
            a. Failure to wait for Samuel (13:8-10).
            b. Foolish vow and intention with Jonathan.
            c. Failure to destroy the Amalekites.
        2. The evil results.
            a. Jealousy toward David.
            b. Thrice-repeated attempted murder.
            c. Inability to keep any resolution.
    C. An awful ending.
        1. Depression, despondency, despair.
        2. Visit to the witch and its implications.
        3. Suicide on battlefield (31:4).

II. **The Cause of His Conduct**
    A. Note his actions.
        1. No real worship at time of anointing.
        2. Impatience at time of waiting.
        3. Foolish stubbornness in incident with Jonathan.
        4. Disobedience with Amalekites.
    B. Attitudes.
        1. Blameshifting (13:11; 15:15; 15:24).
        2. Self-will (serving God until a cost).
        3. Concern with appearances (15:30).
        4. Distrust and jealousy.
        5. Superstition.
        6. Violence and disorder.
    C. Basic issue.
        1. He simply was not a spiritual man.

2. God gave him a new heart; he didn't give God the heart he already had.
   3. He was typical of all uncommitted Christians (those who never really have a heart for God but live on the fringe of Christianity).

III. **The Caution of His Conduct**
   A. Don't live out from under the umbrella of God's protection.
   B. Don't live where God may have to do something extreme to get your attention.
   C. Don't get out of touch with God's specific will for your life.
   D. Don't make foolish assumptions.
      1. "I can break out of this any time I want."
      2. "I will get more spiritual later on."
   E. Don't live a life that leads to great misery.
   F. Don't assume backsliding will end up where you wish—backslidden Christians commit suicide, become immoral, steal money, set fires, etc.

Conclusion

Anyone can go the way of Saul!!! That's right! Anyone can go that way. Saul went the way of the uncommitted, unspiritual, indifferent person. You can go this way, or you can give your heart to God.

Samuel's Swan Song
2 Samuel 12:1-25

Introduction
In this passage Samuel lays aside some of the responsibilities he has carried. He is not retiring, but he is moving to a different role, and he will be part of the story for a while yet. These are his formal remarks at the transference of power.

I. **A Message of Exoneration (vv. 1-5)**
   A. I have done what you have asked.
   B. The situation is thus.
      1. The king is in place.
      2. I am old and grayheaded.
      3. My sons are with you.
      4. I have been in public life since my childhood.
   C. Now judge my integrity.
      1. Deals with a variety of issues.
      2. At least some measure of contrast with king.
      3. Provides excellent example for Saul.
   D. He is exonerated.
      1. People find no fault in him.
      2. Samuel calls God as witness and thus illustrates important principle: right is its own reward.

II. **A Message of Exposition (vv. 6-15)**
   A. "Stand still that I may reason with you" (true religion always has reason on its side).
   B. Does historical review.
      1. Moses, Aaron and the Exodus (vv. 6, 8).
      2. The judges (vv. 9-11).
      3. Recent events (vv. 12, 13) pressure from Nahash had contributed to request for king.
   C. Two summary principles.
      1. Following the Lord has its own reward—to be after the Lord (v. 14).
      2. If we will not have the Lord as ruler, then we will have the Lord as judge (v. 15)

III. **A Message of Exhortation (vv. 16-25)**
   A. A warning about pragmatism (vv. 16-19) [the idea that something is right if it "works"].
      1. They had demanded king and had been warned of consequences—now had king and victory.
      2. Samuel called down thunder (season that it did not usually happen).

3. Thunderstorm showed.
   a. That Samuel had power with God.
   b. That God's anger would be the same against them as against the Philistines (7:10).
   c. That God is more powerful than any king.
   d. That the serenity of life can easily be broken.
   e. That pragmatism is wrong.
B. Assurance concerning their situation (vv. 20-25).
   1. Don't despair (v. 22) God won't give up on you—He didn't choose you because good; He won't drop you because bad.
   2. Don't turn aside (vv. 20, 21) There is no place else to turn.
   3. Don't worry about me (v. 23).
   4. Don't be fooled—Fear the Lord—Show it by service.

Conclusion

When you do turn away from the Lord, He still loves you. Don't turn away, however, because it seems better or because something else seems to have the answers. It will never be better than with Him.

Jonathan: The Man Who Defines Character

1 Samuel 18, 19, 20

Introduction

The slaying of Goliath involves incredible drama, but another incredible drama began that day, the friendship of David and Jonathan. Jonathan is an interesting personality. He was son of Saul, who was king. He was the oldest son and thus "heir apparent." He was a far superior man to his father. He was a towering figure in history, and here's why:

I. **He Valued Right Above Relationship**
   A. He honored friend above father.
      1. Nothing between him and David but friendship.
      2. Frequently defended David to Saul.
      3. Always based arguments on right (cf. 19:4, 5).
   B. This is a rebuking position.
      1. Right always takes precedence over relationship.
      2. We tend to prefer right until it involves relationship.
      3. Standing for right depends on depth of commitment to right.

II. **He Valued Revelation Above Reign**
   A. Jonathan resolved conflict.
      1. He knew he was heir-apparent.
      2. He knew God had chosen David (18:4; 20:31).
      3. God's revealed will settled the conflict for him.
   B. This is an instructive position.
      1. Revelation always conquers.
      2. We tend to accept revelation until it involves some price.
      3. Depth of our commitment to revelation so important.

III. **He Valued Responsibility Before Refuge**
   A. Jonathan made a difficult choice.
      1. Had many options open to him.
      2. Chose to stick with his father.
      3. Paid for decision with life, but stood by responsibility.
   B. This is a searching position.
      1. Responsibility more important than our own well-being.
      2. Easy to stand in safety; retreat in time of danger.
      3. Involves prior commitment to responsibility.

Conclusion

Jonathan really had character, and he provides a model for us.

Character is not developed in crisis; it is merely shown in crisis. Character is developed in the course of life by the countless daily decisions we make.

Would you:
- Value right above relationship?
- Value revelation above reign?
- Value responsibility above refuge?

You may have opportunity to do so even today.

David's Great Sin
2 Samuel 11:1-5

Introduction

We enter one of the bleakest sections of Scripture and feel we are in a dark and swampy area. We tread softly here with sorrow for we cannot come away from this chapter without wondering what ever happened to David.

I. **Note His Previous Character**
   A. Great strength.
      1. In restraint with Saul.
      2. In patience with Ishbosheth.
      3. In military prowess.
   B. Great piety.
      1. Shown in references to Lord.
      2. Shown in keeping vows.
      3. Shown in seeking guidance from God.
   C. Great personal character.
      1. Concern for parents.
      2. Remembering former kindnesses.
      3. Ability to organize loose confederation into great nation.

II. **Note the Extent of His Fall**
   A. Adultery.
   B. Deceit.
      1. Tries to use Uriah to cover his sins.
      2. Even descends to getting him drunk.
   C. Murder.

III. **Note the Possible Explanations**
   A. Merely a matter of falling to temptation.
      1. There are moments when we all are tempted.
      2. Any man can fall—no one is immune.
      3. This is what happened to David.
   B. Does not really answer the question.
      1. Joseph faced same temptation and stood.
      2. His was worse and more fraught with peril.
      3. We have to look deeper for causes.
   C. Internal digression had paved the way—His action was result of previous internal problems.
      1. Established a harem (polygamy).
      2. Failed to cultivate spiritual stamina.
      3. Allowed wrong thought patterns to develop as is seen by later actions.

       4. Took ease at an improper time (should have been at war).
       5. Considered temptation favorably (saw and continued to look).

IV. Note the Lessons
   A. External falls begin with internal deterioration.
       1. No man falls suddenly.
       2. Sins of mind and heart are of tragic consequences.
   B. Shows importance of two Scriptures.
       1. Proverbs 4:23.
       2. Matthew 5:27-28.
   C. No one is exempt from possibility of fall.
       1. Men fall into sin of their own choice.
       2. The fall is a result of a process.

Conclusion

What is going on in your life that could cause you to fall like David? The time to deal with spiritual failure is before it happens.

Adonijah: Going My Way
1 Kings 1:5-9

Introduction

While David was King, Israel rose to great heights, but he sinned with Bathsheba. Ever after that, his own household was in a constant state of disarray. When 1 Kings begins, he is getting old (before his time). God has already declared that He wants Solomon as king, but Adonijah decides to short-circuit God.

I. **The Character of Rebellion**
   A. He had a measure of claim to the throne—he was the oldest living son.
   B. He made a choice and implemented it.
      1. He set himself against the choice and will of God.
      2. He followed almost exactly in the example of Absalom.
   C. One sin led to another.
      1. He exalted himself.
      2. He rebelled against God.
   D. Anything that goes counter to the revealed will of God is:
      1. Exaltation of self.
      2. Rebellion against God.

II. **The Cause of Rebellion**
   A. There are two clues to his rebellion.
      1. He was a "goodly" (beautiful) person.
      2. He had never been restrained.
   B. Teaches us important lessons about rebellion.
      1. Much rebellion springs from too much permissiveness in childhood.
      2. Rebellion becomes a pattern of life that is hard to break in adulthood.

III. **The Confirmation of Rebellion**
   A. He picked up some allies.
      1. He got military leader Joab and co-priest Abiathar.
      2. Each of those who rallied to him had his own reasons for doing so.
   B. Rebellion never wants for its allies. We can always find support for doing wrong.
      1. He looked where he knew he would find support.
      2. There are always "vicarious rebels" just waiting for a rebel to support.
      3. Rebels seek to find support rather than seeking to determine right and wrong.

IV. The Curse of Rebellion
  A. The will of God prevailed, as it always must.
  B. His friends abandoned him when the tables turned (cf. v. 49).
  C. He dealt with his act of rebellion but not with his rebellious spirit.
  D. He died for his sin.

Conclusion

This story shows the importance of restraining self-will and refraining from permissiveness. It shows the danger of rebellion and the deadliness of its results, and it shows the choice we face and the curse we can suffer.

Solomon: Not Fully After the Lord
1 Kings 3:11-14; 4:29-34; 11:1-8

Introduction

The course of Solomon's life is incredible—there is no sadder story of decline than that traced here. Few people have ever slipped from greater heights. Two references here tell us a great deal.

I. **Solomon Demonstrates a Problem**
   A. He did evil in the sight of the Lord.
      1. Much of it is detailed here.
      2. Evidently gradually developed.
   B. He did not go fully after the Lord.
      1. Something had happened in his heart.
      2. As a result, there were reservations in his approach to life.

II. **Solomon Reveals a Process**
   A. Two things always go together.
      1. Wrong actions and conduct.
      2. Backsliding in heart.
   B. The second one listed here always comes first.
      1. Something happens inside before anything goes wrong outside.
      2. Why we are told, "keep thy heart with all diligence; for out of it are the issues of life" (Prov. 4:23).
   C. The first problem always results from the second.
      1. When the heart slips, something always happens as a result.
      2. Impossible to grow cold of heart without specific results in conduct.

III. **Solomon Thus Identifies Principles**
   A. Backsliding always starts in the heart.
      1. Something slips within before anything shows without.
      2. The heart moves and drifts ever so easily.
   B. Backsliding always results in actions.
      1. Sooner or later thinking translates into doing.
      2. When heart is not "perfect toward God," actions tend to line up with the thinking.
   C. Backsliding always ends in trouble.
      1. May take long time to come as God gives opportunity to repent.
      2. Sooner or later, God moves against backsliding.

Conclusion

The backslider has always pulled back from where he was, and he always has his reasons. The backslider will have increasing problems until he gets right with the Lord. Beware—there are two places where we are likely to slip:
- The very bad situation and surroundings.
- The very good situation (Solomon).

How is your heart toward the Lord?

Jeroboam the Determined
1 Kings 11:26—14:20

Introduction

Jeroboam was not a son of Solomon. He was a soldier who caught Solomon's eye and was given a lot of responsibility.

I. **Jeroboam's Golden Opportunity**
   A. The message of the prophet (11:29-39).
      1. Sin of Solomon to be punished.
      2. As a result he was to be given ten tribes.
   B. God intended to do good for Jeroboam (v. 38).
      1. He merely had to obey like David.
      2. God promised him a dynasty.

II. **Jeroboam's Failure**
   A. Kingdom came to him through folly of Solomon's son, Rehoboam.
      1. He was able to establish kingdom.
      2. Had everything going for him then.
   B. He failed miserably.
      1. Established rival worship (12:25-33).
      2. Became a by-word for evil ("sins of Jeroboam" mentioned more than 12 times).
   C. He suffered personal and political loss.
      1. Lost a child.
      2. Died without leaving a dynasty.
      3. God wanted to make him great; he insisted on being mediocre.

III. **Jeroboam's Lessons**
   A. He failed because he wouldn't heed godly counsel (Ahijah; 3:1-3).
      1. We won't listen to what others try to tell us, even if it is from God's Word.
      2. We stand to lose much by failure to heed counsel.
   B. He failed because he wouldn't learn from the example of others.
      1. He had Solomon graphically before him (11:1-8) and was also aware of Rehoboam.
      2. We fail to learn from example of others.
         a. See problems in parents' lives and reproduce them.
         b. Reproduce in children the very things that caused our problems.
   C. He failed because he wouldn't profit from God's dealings in his own life (13:4-10).

1. He witnessed a mighty sign from God but remained unmoved.
2. We do the same—God lays His hand on us, we are momentarily changed, but we are unable to see cause/effect, and we revert.
D. He failed because he simply would not obey God's commands.
1. This was absolutely crucial to his knowing God's blessing.
2. This is likely the largest problem we face in seeing God's hand in our lives.

Conclusion

Jeroboam was a man God wanted to bless, offered to bless, promised to bless, but he was determined to avoid that blessing. God wants to bless you; why are you determined to avoid His blessing?

Elijah and God's Tender, Loving Care
1 Kings 19:4-18

Introduction

Elijah's fainting fit has a note of encouragement for us because God's dealing with him at that time sounds a note that we need to hear.

I. **The Problem**
   A. Physical exhaustion and spiritual disappointment combine at one time.
   B. Satan takes advantage of the opportunity thus afforded to him.
   C. The result is depression so severe that it led to despair.

II. **The Provision**
   A. God let him sleep—it seems to be what he needed most at this juncture.
   B. God then woke him up and fed him.
   C. God sent an angel to minister to him in his need.
   D. God allowed him to express his grief without giving him what he thought he wanted.
   E. God revealed Himself and His ways to him (vv. 11, 12).
   F. God revealed good news to him (vv. 15-18).
   G. God gave him more work to do (v. 16).
   H. God reassured him of His love (v. 18).

III. **The Practicalities**
   A. Notice God's patience.
      1. Elijah knew better than to do what he did.
      2. God still has patience with him.
      3. God has patience with our follies.
   B. God fully understood his infirmity.
      1. He knew what caused the situation.
      2. He knew what was necessary to heal the situation.
   C. We ought to deal with others as God deals with us.
      1. Others fail us as Elijah failed God.
      2. We have the example of how to handle such failure.
      3. When we have no patience with faltering and failure, we set ourselves above God.
   D. Failure doesn't spell end of usefulness.
      1. Some failures may leave scars that limit our usefulness, but it is not eliminated.

       2. We need to get our focus off the past.
  E. Never give up in the midst of bad circumstances and trouble—there are yet good things in store.

Conclusion

There is much of encouragement in Elijah's failure and in God's handling of it. It is easy to lose sight of God in the dark, but it is helpful to remember that He never loses sight of us no matter how dark the night. Just remember Elijah and keep on going no matter what may happen.

Elisha: Let Thy Mantle Fall on Me
1 Kings 19:19-21

Introduction

How would you feel if you were outside shoveling snow or mowing the lawn some evening, and a strange, rough-hewn character should come down the street, take a funny looking skin stole off his shoulders, drop it over yours and then walk away? That's exactly what happened to Elisha.

I. **The Individuals in the Story**
   A. Elijah.
      1. Rough-hewn country boy from poor region.
      2. Almost nothing known of his background.
      3. Ministry one of stern denunciation and judgment.
   B. Elisha.
      1. Strong, rugged man from well-to-do farm family.
      2. Considerable background given in text.
      3. Ministry appears more concerned with people.
   C. Contrasts and similarities.
      1. Many surface dissimilarities.
      2. Essential sameness—same purposes and goals.
      3. Shows.
         a. God calls all different kinds of people.
         b. God calls different kinds of people to the same ministry.
         c. God's call is God's enablement—personality types, etc., do not matter.

II. **The Invitation That Was Extended**
   A. Its form.
      1. The mantle was a symbol of the office.
      2. Placing the mantle on Elisha showed that he was to serve and eventually replace Elijah.
      3. It was done at God's direction (v. 16).
   B. Its circumstances.
      1. Elisha was ploughing.
      2. God's clear calls most often come to those who are busy doing what they have to do
   C. Its lessons.
      1. Every child of God has a call (John 15:16).
      2. God desires to make His call known.
      3. Best way to be sure of God's call is to get busy with what one knows he should be doing.

III. The Impression of the Invitation
   A. Recognition.
      1. Elisha knew the sign and what it meant.
      2. Elisha also knew what it would involve.
   B. Reaction.
      1. He ran after Elijah.
      2. He asked for time to say good-bye to his family.
   C. Reminders.
      1. The man who wants to do God's will and desires to know it will recognize it when it comes.
      2. Our response to God's call ought to be immediate and complete.

IV. The Indication of His Response
   A. His action.
      1. Took the oxen and sacrificed them.
      2. Burned the implements of the oxen.
      3. Had a farewell feast for everyone.
   B. His attitude.
      1. He was burning his bridges.
      2. He was breaking his ties.
   C. His example.
      1. When God calls, we need to burn bridges and go.
      2. Elisha weighed the cost and paid the price. Many people miss blessings because they are afraid of or unwilling to pay a price.

V. The Identification With Elijah
   A. His two-fold response.
      1. He arose and followed Elijah.
      2. He ministered to him.
   B. His revealed character.
      1. He followed an uncertain direction because God said so.
      2. He was content to minister to another.
   C. His practical lessons.
      1. It doesn't have to be "Big" to be God's call.
      2. It is not wrong to follow a man who follows God.
      3. God's call may lead into danger—the only thing more dangerous is failing to heed His call.

Conclusion

God has a plan for everyone, but God shows His will to people busy doing what they know to do and people willing to do His will.

Ahab the Average
I Kings 20, 21

Introduction

I dislike cold things warm, and I dislike warm things cold. I am godly on this score (Rev. 3:15-16). Lukewarmness seems typical of our day but not only of ours. Ahab seems to teach about lukewarmness also.

I. The Case of Ahab—not convinced he was all bad
   A. Did some good.
      1. Impressed by contest on Carmel.
      2. Open to good counsel (20:7-9).
      3. Willing to do things God's way (20:13-15).
      4. Generous to Benhadad (20:31-34).
      5. Repented at rebuke of Elijah (21:27-29).
   B. Did much bad.
      1. Was wrong in generosity to Benhadad (did not listen to the Lord).
      2. Acted like little child in relation to Naboth's vineyard (21:4).
      3. Allowed Jezebel to do wrong with Naboth.
      4. Was delighted with getting his own way.

II. The Curse of Ahab
   A. God cursed him.
      1. For not listening in regard to Benhadad.
      2. For allowing Jezebel to kill Naboth.
   B. He had a greater curse.
      1. He was neither all bad or all good.
      2. He was whatever the strongest pull around him was.
      3. He had no deep commitment to anything but himself.
   C. Ahab is an extreme example of what is condemned in Revelation 3.

III. The Challenge of Ahab
   A. Ahab's lack of commitment made him prey to every influence around him.
      1. His evil nature made him more prey to evil.
      2. This kept him in constant trouble.
   B. Lack of commitment gets us in trouble.
      1. We lack commitment so we lack intensity.
      2. Lack of intensity makes us prey to everything and anything (sin, failure, indifference, apostasy).

C. Our greatest need is a great cause, and God has given us some (e.g. Gal. 4:17, 18).

Conclusion

It greatly bothers me when God's people become lethargic and unconcerned. Does it bother you? Don't be "average;" you may end up like Ahab.

Jabez: A Man More Honorable
1 Chronicles 4:9, 10

Introduction

Here is all we know about a man named Jabez: the meaning of his name, the reason for his name, and that he was exalted above others. Why does he stand out? He prayed, God granted his request, and that made him great.

I. **He Requested the Blessing of God**
   A. "Enlarge my coast"—material blessings of more land or greater possessions.
   B. Wanted what God and only God could give.
      1. "Oh that Thou wouldest bless me indeed."
      2. Used name of covenant God here.
   C. What is there in your life that could not be there if it were not for God?

II. **He Required the Presence of God**
   A. "That thine hand might be with me"—that thy hand might be upon my life.
   B. Wanted God in every area of life—his desire was to be bound up with God in the bundle of life.
   C. How much do we really want God in all of our lives?

III. **He Recognized the Danger of Sin**
   A. "That thou wouldst keep me from evil".
      1. Broader than, but including sin.
      2. Wanted to be kept from sinning.
   B. Had reason for this request.
      1. That it might not grieve me—cause me problems.
      2. Recognized important truth—sin grieves God, others, and ourselves. To watch Christians, one would never know that sin grieves.

Conclusion

He, coming before, learned truths that we, coming after, miss.
- That real prosperity comes only through the blessing of God.
- That His will and presence are the most important things in life.
- That sin and evil are a grief.

He prayed, God answered, and he was more honorable than his brethren. Are you? How did you get so?

John the Baptist: Man, Ministry, Message
Mark 1:1-15

Introduction

There are two very prominent New Testament men named John. One is John the Baptist (the baptizer); the other is John the Apostle. They are very different people (trace differences).

I. **John the Baptist—The Man**
   A. Christ's opinion of him (Matt. 11:11).
   B. His greatness consisted of:
      1. Humility.
      2. Dedication to his task.
      3. Conformity to the will of God.
   C. He provides an example.

II. **John the Baptist—The Ministry**
   A. Had specific task.
      1. Warn nation of true character of the coming kingdom.
      2. Prepare hearts for the reception of the Gospel.
   B. His was a secondary, subordinate role.
   C. There is a place for such roles even today.

III. **John the Baptist—The Message**
   A. Strictly preparatory.
   B. Illustrated by his baptism.
      1. His baptism was different from Christian baptism.
      2. Those he baptized were baptized again (Acts 19:1-7).
      3. This shows that something was missing.
   C. Typical of our day—many people have a John Baptist concept of salvation.

Conclusion

John the Baptist had his bad moments (while in jail), but Christ puts him in perspective. Note last part of Matthew 11:11—the one who knows Christ is way ahead of John the Baptist, who only represented part of the picture.

Good King Hezekiah
2 Chronicles 31:20, 21

Introduction

By and large, 2 Chronicles is a depressing book. With rare exception, it is the story of decline and rebellion against God, but one of those rare exceptions was Hezekiah. Hezekiah was different, and in his differentness there is something for us to learn.

I. **The Ministry of Hezekiah**
   A. He was the son of a bad father, but he did not follow in his ways.
   B. He instituted—almost from the moment he took the throne—religious reforms.
      1. Restored the priesthood to its proper function.
      2. Cleansed the house of God.
      3. Reinstituted the sacrifices.
      4. Resumed the observances—Passover.
      5. Saw to it that the Word was taught.
   C. As a result of the religious reforms, there were many social and civil reforms effected as well.

II. **The Manner of Hezekiah**
   A. What he did, he did with all his heart.
      1. He was characterized by a total commitment.
      2. When he decided to do something, he put his whole heart into it.
   B. From observing his life, we can see what wholeheartedness is like.
      1. Thinking earnestly for the Lord.
      2. Doing something about problems rather than just observing or bemoaning them.
      3. Doing what one has resolved to do.
      4. Maintaining perseverance.
      5. Depending on God in constant prayer for his Help and strength.

III. **The Motivation of Hezekiah**
   A. The greatest of work to do.
      1. He touched heaven and earth.
      2. We also touch heaven and earth—never more so than when we deal with souls.
   B. The effectiveness of Satan.
      1. He is a constantly worthy opponent.
      2. One of his primary methods is half-heartedness.

- C. The responsibility that goes with being in a particular situation.
    1. Belief in will of God should lead to conviction that we are where we are by the direction of the Lord.
    2. We are on assignment from the king—better do a good job.
- D. The fact that we deal with the souls of men gives us even greater incentive than Hezekiah had.
- E. The stream of death constantly washing away men.
    1. Constantly reminded of this by news.
    2. We need a sense of urgency.
- F. The love of Christ.
    1. His love to us is the example.
    2. The life of Christ provides an example of the whole-hearted servant.
- G. The logic of what we owe.
    1. We have an non-repayable debt.
    2. We ought to be doing something toward paying that debt.

Conclusion

Hezekiah did what he did with all his heart. As a result, he prospered in whatever he did. Are you a "whole-heart" or a "half-heart"?

Josiah the Tenderhearted
2 Chronicles 34, 35

Introduction

Some people seem able to do much with little. They make great use of small abilities, make great things with few resources, and make outstanding lives out of small endowments. Josiah was one of these people.

I. **Josiah's Start**
   He had so much going against him.
   A. Ancestry.
      1. Grandfather was very evil (33:9).
      2. Father even worse [forgot grandfather's brief revival] (33:22, 23).
   B. Half-orphaned at early age.
   C. Came to throne when way too young.
   D. Was surrounded by father's evil advisors and courtesans.
   E. Came at very bad time in Judah's history.

II. **Josiah's Success**
   A. Succeeded in temporary turn of nation.
   B. Restored religion.
      1. Brought it back to proper place.
      2. Brought it back to proper observance (35:18).
   C. Rated best king to sit on throne of Judah (see 2 Kings 23:25).
      1. May not include David and Solomon.
      2. May include David and Solomon as he was better than each in some ways.

III. **Josiah's Secret**
   A. Readily identified (2 Kings 22:19 and 2 Chron. 34:27)—He had a tender heart toward the Lord.
   B. Detailed.
      1. He was concerned about the things of God (from early youth).
      2. He was committed to the service of God (started work on temple when 16).
      3. He was conformed to the Word of God.
         a. Unusual revival.
         b. Conformed to Word as soon as he knew what it said.
      4. He was concerned with a personal relationship with God (dealt with sin as soon as aware of it).

5. He was interested in the well-being of God's people (viewed their sin as his).
6. He was dedicated to doing things the very best for God.
  C. Applied.
    1. What kind of person should a ministry produce?
    2. A person with tender heart to God.
    3. There are three enemies to this: self, society, Satan.

Conclusion

Josiah was a grand success, and Josiah was tender-hearted to God. Don't you want a heart that is tender toward the Lord?

Ezra: The Man With the Right Heart
Ezra 7:1-28

Introduction

A new actor comes on stage in the midst of this book, and he is worth a look, because he is quite a man. Actually Ezra is one of the giants of the Bible.

I. **The Magnitude of the Man**
   A. Had great prominence with heathen king.
      1. Shown.
         a. His requests granted (v. 7).
         b. Power of inquiry (v. 14).
         c. Entrusted with riches (v. 15-20).
         d. Access to king's treasury (vv. 21, 22).
         e. Granted tax exemption (v. 24).
         f. Given magisterial authority (vv. 25, 26) including death penalty.
      2. Answers question, "When is it all right to have the respect of the ungodly?" When it comes without seeking or compromise.
   B. Had enormous personal power or influence.
      1. Got others to go with him.
      2. Was able to stir decadent people.
   C. Had deep courage.
      1. Refused armed guard for journey.
      2. Faced delicate separation issue.
   D. Had profound spiritual impact.
      1. Effected real reforms.
      2. Brought about a measure of revival.
   E. Had touch of God on his life.
      1. Continually speaks of, "The good hand of the Lord upon me."
      2. This is the element without which all else is totally meaningless.

II. **The Making of the Man**
   A. The crucial issue he faced: "Ezra prepared his heart."
      1. Had cleansed his heart before God.
      2. Had received a heart purpose from God.
   B. The crucial knowledge he had (Prov. 4:23).
      1. God knows what is in the heart (Ps. 139:1-12).
      2. God can punish what is in it (Matt. 5:27, 28).
      3. One's attitude comes out of it (Prov. 23:7).

        4. One's actions spring from it (Matt. 12:24; 15:19).
        5. One's happiness depends on it (Isa. 65:14).
    C. The crucial stance he took.
        1. Ezra was a "whole-heart."
        2. Shown in various ways throughout his life.

III. The Manner of the Man
    A. He sought the law—knowledge.
        1. Ezra knew future seat of spiritual worship was a book and not a building.
        2. No possibility of ever having a right heart without the Book.
    B. He sought to do it—obedience.
        1. Knowledge of law useless without life application.
        2. Practicing teaching of the Word will keep heart pure.
        3. There can not be a right heart without obedience.
    C. He sought to share it with others—teaching.
        1. His teaching was based on knowledge and obedience.
        2. We all have an obligation to teach.
    D. He clearly recognized God—gratitude.
        1. Gave God credit for everything.
        2. A right heart always gives God the glory.

Conclusion

Ezra was a giant of a man. He didn't get that way by accident. The key to his stature was a right heart.

The Rich Young Ruler
Mark 10:17-22; 1 Timothy 6:6-10, 17-19

Introduction

The Bible is full of pictures of men. Many of them are much like men today because human nature doesn't change. Let's meet a man who has many counterparts today.

I. **Meet the Man**
   A. He was young.
      1. Matthew 19:20.
      2. Must have been near thirty as Luke 18:18 shows.
   B. He was rich.
      1. Never has there been a richer land than ours.
      2. Luke 18:23; Matthew 19:23.
   C. He was very moral.
      1. Exemplary character (v. 20).
      2. Seemed to feel that morality was not enough.
   D. He was religious.
      1. He knew the Old Testament and practiced it.
      2. Coming to Christ shows interest in spiritual things.
   E. He demonstrated promise.
      1. Probably nice personality, etc.
      2. Mark 10:21 says Christ "loved" (desired) him.

II. **Examine His Problem**
   A. He was trusting in the wrong things.
      1. Trusting in money, morality, and works.
      2. Shows that doing good is not enough, for he did a great deal.
   B. He lacked assurance.
      1. There is never assurance when faith is not in the Lord.
      2. He was an honest seeker.
   C. He loved his money more than he desired eternal things.
      1. Asked about eternal life.
      2. Turned away when told to give all goods to poor.
      3. Doing so would have been a sign of the genuine faith which he actually lacked.
      4. It also showed him to be a liar in his protestations of concern for fellow man.

III. **Give Him the Answer**
   A. Christian contentment (1 Tim. 6:6-10).
      1. Could have found this in Christ.
      2. Comes with a proper realization of relative values.

       3. Realization of the fact that money causes much trouble when it is loved too much.
  B. Eternal investments (1 Tim. 6:17-19).
       1. Things of God are of first importance.
       2. First obligation in verse 18.
       3. Such living carries on beyond this life.

Conclusion

Here is a man who met Christ but was kept from knowing him by self-trust and love of material things. Many Christians are kept from really drawing close to Him by a love of the material. Many people are kept from coming to Him by the appeal of material things.

Simeon's Spiritual Secrets
Luke 2:21-38

Introduction

Although we do not know much about Simeon, what we do know is significant.

I. **Simeon's Spiritual State**
   A. "Man" in Jerusalem—not priest or official.
   B. High spiritual character.
      1. Righteous—upright.
      2. Devout—earnest.
      3. Waiting for consolation of Israel.
   C. Empowered by Holy Spirit.
      1. Holy Spirit was upon him (v. 25).
      2. Holy Spirit had revealed to him (v. 26).
      3. Holy Spirit led him (v. 27).
   D. Given specific promise from God (v. 26). (Most likely because of his piety.)

II. **Simeon's Spiritual Secrets**
   A. Salvation is in a person (v. 30).
      1. Almost every religion has a salvation.
      2. Almost all are found in some thing or some act.
      3. Christianity's salvation is in a person—Jesus Christ.
      4. Until you know that person, you do not know salvation.
   B. Salvation is for everyone (vv. 31, 31).
      1. Jewish exclusivism was prevalent.
      2. Simeon makes a truly comprehensive statement.
      3. Salvation is open to all—no condition on it.
   C. Salvation brings divisions and problems (vv. 34, 35*a*).
      1. Specific statements.
         a. He will cause a division in Israel—some will fall while others will rise.
         b. He will cause offense and be much spoken against.
         c. He will cause you grief and sorrow.
      2. Special significance.
         a. Wherever Christ and salvation go, divisions are created.
         b. Christ is still spoken against; so will we be.
         c. He created divisions; so will we when we stand for Him.

      D. Salvation allows a peaceful departure (v. 29).
          1. Interpretation.
              a. "Please let me go."
              b. "In peace"—a statement of fact, not part of request.
          2. Only Christianity allows knowledgeable peaceful departure.
              a. Others may go peacefully, but it has no basis.
              b. Must know Christ to go peacefully.
      E. Salvation a revealer of hearts.
          1. Christ saw through people and revealed them.
          2. Everyone who touched Christ was revealed.
          3. Gospel becomes great revealer.

III. **Simeon's Spiritual Stress**
      A. Saw the enormous significance of Christ.
      B. Saw the cruciality of salvation.
      C. Saw that salvation is in a person.

Conclusion

    Do you know Simeon's spiritual secrets? The first is the key to all the rest: salvation is in a person. Do you know Him?

The Prodigal Son
Luke 15

Introduction
Here is an interesting and complex young man.

I. **He Was Tremendously Short-sighted (vv. 12, 13)**
   A. Request for inheritance doubtlessly was not first step of apostasy.
      1. Likely began long before request was made.
      2. Stayed around a while after division—to give appearance of piety?
   B. Major backsliding seldom happens suddenly.
      1. Small steps are taken first.
      2. Be careful if you have begun to go backward.

II. **He Was Deeply Self-centered (vv. 12, 13)**
   A. Shown in his request.
      1. "Father, give me."
      2. Give me what is *mine* (saw father's gift as father's debt).
   B. Shown in its granting.
      1. Father divided his "living"—what he took reduced what his father had (likely he got one third of all).
      2. His selfishness shows starkly against his father's generosity.

III. **He Was Absolutely Self-willed (vv. 12-14*a*, 15)**
   A. He said, "I'll do it my way."
      1. Took the attitude that his father was keeping from him something that was good.
      2. Probably was also weary of his father's rules.
   B. He went to a "far country."
      1. Rebels always want to put space between themselves and authorities.
      2. Seen in backsliders out of church—runaways.
   C. He joined himself to a citizen of the far country.
   "Departure from the Lord always makes us dependent on others that we were never meant to depend upon."

IV. **He Was Overwhelmingly Sensuous (vv. 13*b*, 14*a*, 30)**
   A. Began when he exchanged the permanent for the immediate.
   B. Became involved in all manner of things.
      1. Wasting substance comes naturally to the self-centered.
      2. Selfishness, rebellion, and sensuousness almost always go together.

    C. He got caught in spiritual inversion.
       1. God's way: good by personal experience; evil by sight or sense.
       2. Devil's way: evil by personal experience, good as the opposite of what he was experiencing.

V. He Was Intensely Stubborn (v. 16)
    A. Caught in process.
       1. "I'll get right when things get a little worse."
       2. Make no attempt to turn back until broken.
    B. Stubbornness usually goes with rebellion and makes it much worse.

VI. He Was Sublimely Sensible at Last (v. 17)
    A. He came to his senses—for the first time.
       1. He was not sane when he left.
       2. He has not been sane since he has been gone.
    B. When he did "come to," he took immediate action.
       1. Didn't wait for things to improve—moved.
       2. No interval between saying and doing.

Conclusion

Story is a mirror—see yourself here? Where are you in it? Only safe thing to reflect is last one. Why not get sensible before you run out of opportunities?

That Older Brother
Luke 15:24-32

Introduction

Look at the older brother—that other one. He is essential to a real understanding of the story of the Prodigal, and he is a characteristic Pharisee. The story could be called "The Anatomy of a Wrong Attitude."

I. **He Did Not Understand Himself Clearly**
   A. He was upset because he didn't get what he wanted.
      1. He could have had it at any time.
      2. He already had two-thirds of inheritance.
   B. He boasted of his own virtue and obedience.
      1. He probably said more than was true—if he was so obedient to and concerned about his father, why was he so obstinate here?
      2. "Those that think too highly of themselves and their services are apt to think hardly of their masters and meanly of their favors".

II. **He Did Not Understand His Father Clearly**
   A. The heart of his misunderstanding.
      1. He was devoted to his father's law and service.
      2. He was entirely out of harmony with his father's heart.
      3. Always a danger that we get so involved in serving God that we forget to have His heart.
   B. His father's goodness did not diminish his own possession—he already had his share of the inheritance.
   C. He revealed his father's love clearly.
      1. Tried to drive a wedge between his brother and his father.
      2. As father had gone to greet brother, now he comes to court elder brother.
   D. We must be careful not to miss God's loving heart in the process of our standards and service.

III. **He Did Not Understand Real Values Clearly**
   A. The cause of his upset.
      1. Nothing special had been done for him.
      2. A wastrel comes back and gets what he didn't get.
   B. The point that he missed.
      1. He was there all the time.
      2. He had the father's love and provision at all times.

    C. The lessons that he teaches.
        1. There is no special virtue in being away and coming back—this man was of equal worth and had avoided all the mess.
        2. God's regular goodness is greater than the miracle—we often get frustrated for lack of a miracle when we have overwhelming evidence of God's regular care.

IV. He Did Not Understand the Nature of Forgiveness
    A. Note his attitude.
        1. Wouldn't be in same house with him.
        2. Wouldn't call him brother (v. 30).
        3. Exaggerated (stressed) his faults.
        4. Grudged him the kindness shown.
    B. Failed to recognize truths.
        1. Father had forgiven him.
        2. He was deeply penitent.
        3. It was the father's business.

Conclusion

We need to be very careful of older brotherism. Beware of pride! Be sure to have the real mind of God. Value relationship with Him highly. Be forgiving.

The point of the parable: The Pharisee is as bad as the Prodigal.

John the Apostle: Old Man of the Faith
John 1:1-14

Introduction

Ever notice how God uses such different people? Four main New Testament characters are so different:
- Peter—impetuous activist.
- Paul—managerial visionary.
- James—conservative traditionalist.
- John—meditative intellectual.

I. **The Story of John**
   A. Known for:
      1. Towering intellect.
      2. Spiritual depth.
      3. Consecrated imagination.
      4. Encompassing love.
   B. Wasn't always like that.
      1. Called "Son of Thunder" with reason (Mark 3:17).
      2. Sometimes vain (Mark 9:38).
      3. Hostile (Luke 9:54).
      4. Self-seeking (Mark 10:35-7).
      5. Generally impetuous and antagonistic.
   C. What made the change?
      1. Only thing we can see is having been with Jesus.
      2. Fits with 2 Corinthians 3:18.

II. **The Contrast of John**
   A. Men changed different ways.
      1. Peter by failure and restoration.
      2. Paul by direct confrontation.
      3. James by resurrection appearance.
      4. John by being with Jesus.
   B. God doesn't deal with everyone the same.

III. **The Lessons From John**
   A. God uses all kinds of people.
   B. God deals with each man individually.
   C. The importance of that dealing cannot be overestimated.

Conclusion

God can use you! Has He dealt with your life? Are you changed? Being with and responding to Jesus are the keys to usefulness.

In the Trail of Thomas
John 20:24-29

Introduction

What a thing to be remembered for—the fact you could doubt as well as anyone! Thomas was a doubter, but we know a few other things about him as well, although our information is limited to four passages.

I. **What He Was Like**
   A. John 11:26.
      1. Thomas was saying, "We might as well all go there and die and get it over with."
      2. Example of a very morose frame of mind.
   B. John 14:5.
      1. Element of impatience, rebuke in this, "We don't know where you are going and how can you expect us to?"
      2. Example of a negative mindset.
   C. John 20:24, 25.
      1. Strong expression of disbelief, "I don't trust you men. I don't believe anything I can't personally experience."
      2. Example of ugliness, sneering unbelief.
   D. John 20:26-29.
      1. Rapid response to reproof (no indication that he even reached out and touched).
      2. Example of faith emerging when there was no other alternative.

II. **What His Problem Was**
   A. Obviously a lack of faith—thus the "doubting Thomas" designation.
   B. More to it than that.
      1. Had failed to observe what had been going on around him.
      2. Was unwilling to see, understand, accept.
      3. Unbelief is a matter of choice or the culmination of a series of choices.

III. **Where the Solution Lies**
   A. He was cured by his encounter with the risen Christ.
   B. The same cure is offered today.
      1. Face things as they are.
      2. Review what Christ has done to this point.
      3. Reset focus on Him.

Conclusion

We excuse unbelief as a matter of weakness or the way we are made (a form of blaming the Lord for it) when it is a matter of personal responsibility. We all have reason enough to believe; unbelief is a form of rebellion. The ultimate rebellion is to seek to be saved some way other than as God has provided.

The Man Born Blind: Now I Can See
John 9:25

Introduction

The man born blind is caught in the middle. The Pharisees are determined to "get" Jesus and seize on the fact that He has done a miracle on the Sabbath. In the midst of the conflict between Pharisees and Christ, the blind man makes an amazing display. He has an incredible testimony.

I. **It Was Experiential**
   A. Something actually happened.
   B. We don't base our testimony on experience, but there should be something that happened.

II. **It Was Obvious**
   A. A change had taken place—he had been blind and was no longer so.
   B. Question reality of decision which produces no change.
   C. Facts are always more stubborn than opinions.

III. **It Was Simple**
   A. He didn't know all that had happened, but he knew something had.
   B. Your most powerful witness-weapon is the fact that something has happened.
   C. You don't need to know much to witness.

IV. **It Was Personal**
   A. This happened to him and not to his parents.
   B. They said, "Ask, he is of age" (v. 21).
   C. Your parents religion has virtually no relation to you.

V. **It Was Open**
   A. He knew he would come under pressure for giving his testimony but spoke regardless.
   B. He actually challenged the Jews (vv. 27, 30-33).
   C. A testimony that is not open is not a testimony.

VI. **It Was Growing**
   A. Note how it progresses in the story.
      1. "A man named Jesus" (v. 11).
      2. "He is a prophet" (v. 17).
      3. "Would ye also become His disciples?" (v. 27).
      4. "If He were not from God, He could not do anything." (v. 33).
      5. "Lord, I believe" (v. 38).

    B. A genuine testimony ought to be growing.
VII. **It Was Costly**
    A. He ended up excommunicated for what he believed.
    B. "If Christianity were a crime, would there be enough evidence to convict you?"

Conclusion

You don't have to know much to give a sterling testimony, but you do need to know for sure that something has happened in your life. Has anything happened in your life? Can you say the same things this man said? Are you sure you have been saved?

Judas: The Man Who Gave Traitors a Bad Name
John 13:21-30

Introduction

People give children all kinds of names, but we seldom hear of one named Judas. "Judas" just has too much infamy about it, but the three biggest problems of Judas are common to most of us to at least some degree.

I. **Judas Missed the Point of Everything**
   A. Right in the midst of the disciples.
      1. He never found salvation.
      2. He never understood who Christ really was.
      3. He never caught on to true meaning of His teaching.
   B. We are guilty of the same thing.
      1. Some miss salvation.
      2. Some miss the good things going on.
      3. Some miss the entire point of what Christianity itself is all about.

II. **Judas Perfected the Art of Hypocrisy**
   A. He was a remarkable man.
      1. Was intimate with disciples for three full years.
      2. Incredible that no one questioned him even at the end.
      3. He was able to fool everyone but two: Christ and himself.
   B. We are sometimes remarkable.
      1. We fool people (although not as much as we often think we do).
      2. We know how to put on all the masks.
      3. We ultimately cannot fool Christ or ourselves.

III. **Judas Missed His Chance at Repentance**
   A. He created a terrible mess but still could have redeemed it.
      1. He recognized that he had created the mess.
      2. He was sorry for the mess he made.
      3. He never repented; he was just sorry.
   B. We have the same problem.
      1. We get ourselves in messes.
      2. We are sorry about the messes.
      3. We never really deal with the sin that is behind the mess.

Conclusion

Do you have continuing problems because you won't deal with the real cause?

Have you perfected the art of hypocrisy?

Are you missing the point of what is going on?

Have you failed to find salvation and now feel you can't do anything about it?

There are powerful lessons to be learned from Judas.

Cornelius: The Missing Ingredient
Acts 10

Introduction

Cornelius was in Caesarea and had a vision. Peter was in Joppa and had a vision. God brought the men together as a result of the visions.

I. **The Man Cornelius**
   A. Was in occupation force—not usually respected.
   B. Note description.
      1. Devout (v. 2)—sincere, earnest.
      2. Feared God (v. 2)—stood in awe, believed in.
      3. With his house (v. 2)—rules house in right direction.
      4. Gave much alms (v. 2)—generous, concerned for others.
      5. Prayed to God always (v. 2).
      6. Just (v. 22)—fair, balanced, upright.
      7. Of good report (v. 22)—excellent reputation.
   C. Summary: Man of sincere religious beliefs and of deep moral convictions and character.

II. **The Need of Cornelius**
   A. Humanly speaking he had all anyone could ask for.
      1. Surely this satisfied man.
      2. Surely this would satisfy God.
   B. Very obvious in story that something is missing.
      1. Important enough for God to act directly.
      2. Important enough for whole chapter in Bible.
      3. God reaches into time to deal with that lack.
   C. Missing ingredient is trusting Christ.
      1. Peter preaches (vv. 38-43).
      2. Key phrase here (v. 43*b*).
      3. Cornelius did just that.

III. **The Lessons From Cornelius**
   A. All the best of things not adequate.
      1. Sincerity is not enough.
      2. Giving is not adequate.
      3. Morality and character will not avail.
      4. Religion is not sufficient—he was as religious as a man could be.
   B. Explains some things.
      1. You may have all of these things and yet sense a deep inadequacy.
      2. It is because something *is* missing.

- C. Provides a great caution.
    1. You may be trusting one of these things.
    2. Very common resting places: sincerity, religiousness, goodness.
    3. None is sufficient.
    4. You, too, must trust Christ.

Conclusion

The story of Cornelius exposes a raw nerve of missing ingredients: if you sense an emptiness, nothing new will fill it, but Christ. Only Christ is the answer.

Timothy: The Really Important Things
1 Timothy 4:12

Introduction
By today's standards, thirty-eight years old isn't very young, but it was different in Paul's day. That's about how old Timothy was at this time, and Paul is so concerned that his youth would be a problem that he writes him about it.

I. **A Responsible Man for a Demanding Job**
   A. Timothy had significant responsibilities.
      1. Actually an apostolic emissary.
      2. Overseeing sizable church.
      3. Probably had many older than he under him.
   B. "Let no man despise thy youth"—live in such a way that no one can make issue of age or of experience.
   C. May have a message for today—too much, too soon?

II. **A Reasonable Model for Needed Roles**
   A. "Be thou an example."
      1. Implies that he should be an example.
      2. Truth is that he was an example; so are you to someone no matter who you are.
      3. Better to speak of "good" example.
   B. Actually calling upon him to be a role-model.
      1. He should live as he would want followers to live.
      2. His leadership would be strengthened by his life.

III. **A Requiring List of Crucial Roles**
   Areas selected for development of model leadership indicate that they are crucial to successful Christian leadership.
   A. In word—the things you say.
      1. Words have enormous power.
      2. Words are great revealers (of what is inside).
      3. Words are significant indicators of what is going on inside.
   B. In conversation—early English word for manner of life.
      1. Has to do with the entire way you live.
      2. Every aspect of life is watched.
      3. Brings to mind Philippians 1:27.
   C. In love—meeting needs on deepest level.
      1. We are to love our "loved ones"—husbands/wives.
      2. We are to love the brethren.
      3. We are to love our neighbors.
      4. We are to love our enemies.

D. In faith.
   1. The things believed.
   2. The ability to believe enough to get things from God.
   3. Believing enough to do what God says.
E. Purity—conformity to the moral law of God.
   1. Far more than just sexual purity, although that is included.
   2. If we gave more attention to the task of general conformity to God's law, we might have fewer moral problems.

Conclusion

These are the areas in which Timothy was to provide a model. They are crucial to spiritual life, and they are crucial to spiritual success. Do you want your children, followers, employees, etc. to do what you are doing? It is time to get things sorted out in life!